WENDELL BARNES

I.R.E.C.O.G.N.I.Z.E.

Copyright © 2022 by Wendell Barnes

All rights reserved. No part of this publication may be reproduced, stored or transmitted in any form or by any means, electronic, mechanical, photocopying, recording, scanning, or otherwise without written permission from the publisher. It is illegal to copy this book, post it to a website, or distribute it by any other means without permission.

First edition

This Book is dedicated to the life and memory of my beautiful mother Linda Patricia Darnell, May 20th, 1943-December 29th, 1999.

May you and the ancestors continue to direct and guide me along my journey! I will forever love you momma...My Babydoll!

Ladell Prince Barnes 07/18/1940 - 01/15/1979

I also dedicate this work to my deceased father and nephew both tragically slain early in their lives.

Eric Anthony Woulard Sr.
October 22nd, 1996 – June 16th, 2007

You were my motivation for transformation. My heart has a reserved void from your absence. As your uncle I realize the influence I had on you should've been better. I pray for your forgiveness for my lack of guidance and misdirection. Just know my agency is dedicated to making a positive impact on people's lives.
I love you neffew!

See you in time! I'm goin' hard on 'em!"

Contents

Foreword	iii
Acknowledgement	v
I. R.E.C.O.G.N.I.Z.E.	1
Reflection Section	5
Reflection Notes	6
R. Redirect/Reprogram	7
Reflection Section	10
Reflection Notes	11
E. Envision/Empower	12
Reflection Section	14
Reflection Notes	15
C. Construct/Commit	16
Reflection Section	18
Reflection Notes	19
O. Organize/Objectives	20
Reflection Section	22
Reflection Notes	23
G. Generate/Goals	24
Reflection Section	26
Reflection Notes	27
N. Negotiate/Networks	28
Reflection Section	29
Reflection Notes	30
I. Investigation/Implementation	31
Reflection Section	32
Reflection Notes	33

Z. Zealously/Zero In	34
Reflection Section	35
Reflection Notes	36
E. Emerge/Execute	37
Reflection Section	38
Reflection Notes	39

Foreword

Wendell Barnes is a Returning Citizen of 13 years. Following his release in 2009, Mr. "Win" as he prefers to be called, enrolled in Milwaukee Area Technical College's Human Services program in 2010. While attending college, Win received his ministerial license and ordination under Pastor Michael Champion. In 2013, he earned his Associates Degree. In 2015, Mr. Win opened the first black-owned 24-hour childcare center located in Racine, Wisconsin.

It was while he was working for a community service agency and completing an assignment that Win decided what population he wanted to serve, the most forgotten about; youth who age out of foster care and returning citizens with that in mind Win began building his own portfolio.

A collection of documents that can serve as evidentiary proof of his transformation. He began collecting certificates, honor roll commendations, recognition awards from work and even his Degree from college. Working with youth and certain populations come with barriers based on the offense and occupation one chooses. Such was the case with Mr. Win, he had a lifetime ban on working within certain industries unless he could prove he had been rehabilitated. Mr Win did just that in 2018, after being out of prison for 9 years and 5 years after discharging from supervision, he appeared before the Wisconsin Department of Human Services rehabilitation panel and presented his case. The state of Wisconsin now officially and legally recognized the transformation in Mr. Win by conferring a letter of Approval of Rehabilitation from the Wisconsin DHS.

This module is the direct result of Mr. Win's intentionally documenting the distinct stages and phases he's undergone once he became entangled in the criminal justice system. What is presented here is a condensed version of an extensive self-psychoanalysis of **the criminal thoughts which led to criminal actions which resulted in incarceration!**

I designed this module to work as a course curriculum for the Department of Corrections, for returning citizens, and it is also designed for anyone who feels as though they are lost or stuck in a perpetual cycle of failure and desires to succeed on any level in life. Please read and enjoy.

I confer peace, prosperity, and blessings upon you.

Wendell P. Barnes

Acknowledgement

First of all, I can't proceed without giving honor, praise, thanks, and acknowledgement to that which I call My DIVINE, the Life source energy which connects all life forms. I attribute all knowledge, wisdom and understanding in life to YOU!

Next, without a doubt I must appreciate, thank, and send much love to my foundation, the core, WAWG crew starting with my big little sister Constance Mary Barnes-Griffin for always believing in me even when I couldn't, I thank you for saving my life when I was in the county. Don't think I'll ever forget that among the countless other selfless acts you've shown throughout our lives. Peace wit 2 fingers and One Love from ya bredren.

To Lynn Patrice Barnes, another one of my big sisters, I know we've had difficulties, but please know the love I have for you is eternal. All the conversations, words of encouragement and realness helped me to accomplish my goals. You made me face some harsh realities about myself and I now appreciate the addition to my character. Having you both as my hugest supporters while attending college and going through ministry is how I made it! Even though y'all are my biggest cheerleaders, y'all are ALSO the real MVP's!

Sean Gabriel Montier De La Rosa my lil' bro, you cried the first time I got locked up, and smiled the last time you picked me up. It's been 13 years since that day and now, I'm off paper, a business owner, (you helped with that!) graduated and got published. You pushed me to stay on the straight route and out of the way. I did, and look at us now. N:**a. We made it!!

I would also like to acknowledge my two eldest sisters Karen Jackson and her twin Sharon Munson for their contribution to making this module possible.

My children William Barnes, Arianna Graff, and Brandon Graff, although we're estranged, I pray all is well and someday you realize that I do love you.

I would like to send a special thanks to my former Pastor Michael Champion (Milwaukee, Wisconsin) for always being there for me in times of need. I thank you for being a father figure and a moral compass as I endeavored to change. I thank you for teaching me all that you did. I truly consider you a friend. Anytime you need anything I'm here.

I would be remiss if I didn't acknowledge my soon-to-be ex-wife Serena A Barnes for all of your hard work, dedication, and commitment. Knowingly and oftentimes unknowingly you were the inspiration to complete so many of the plans that I did. Many times we'd argue and fight to come to a resolution. You always challenged me to give my best and I appreciate you for all the encouragement! May the Divine bless your next chapter!

Lastly, but never least, I want to recognize my brother's Adonja Pickett, Shawndell Barnes, Ladell Barnes, sisters Angie Pickett and Kabathia Osborne I love you all, we'll get together soon!

If I forgot to mention you, and you were **part of my success, please charge it to my head and not my heart I'll get you in the next one.**

I. R.E.C.O.G.N.I.Z.E.

Introspection, (from Latin *introspicere*: "to look within"), The process of observing the operations of one's own mind with a view to discovering the laws that govern the mind. In a dualistic philosophy, which divides the natural world (matter, including the human body) from the contents of consciousness, introspection is the chief method of psychology.

I.R.E.C.O.N.I.Z.E. is not only an acronym, but more than that, it is a call for accountability for those that are prepared to take a critical examination of themselves, their positions in life, and the thought processes that navigated them to their present conditions.

This manual was designed with returning citizens in mind, based on statistical data which states: "between 66-82% of individuals released from incarceration end up re-incarcerated within 3-10 years (BJS bjs.ojp.gov)

As a returning citizen and one of those who have been part of that statistic, I am presenting the methodology I implemented to not only get out of the revolving prison doors, but also obtain an Associate's degree, purchase a home, launch several successful businesses, and start a non-profit organization, as well as pursue my passion, writing. What I have written here is based on my personal experience but can be utilized by anyone. It requires us to examine our own thought processes and accept the role that you and I play in our own demise.

I. R.E.C.O.G.N.I.Z.E.

Once we can identify, recognize, and accept that we have some flaws to our thinking processes which are self-defeating, then we can redirect the thought process. This allows us to predetermine the results and anticipated consequences. All consequences, whether good or bad, are a direct result of actions, which are based on thoughts that stem from one's personal belief system. If your goal is to obtain the best results for your life, you **_MUST BE INTENTIONAL!_**

I. Inventory/Identify: I have been incarcerated many times, which was mostly county time, but it was the 5 years of state time in the Wisconsin Department of Corrections that caused me to re-evaluate my choices and decisions. In order to get different results, you must change how you think.

For me, the humiliation of having to strip naked, take a freezing cold crab bath, having racist guards barking orders at me, and restricting my movements should have been enough to make a drunk snake go straight. But like so many others that didn't learn their first time around, I ended up back in prison less than 3 years after my release. Faced with the consequences of my actions, I began to question my own decisions. This is where the initial inventory and identification of the thoughts took place which prompted the actions that resulted in me being reincarcerated. Let me be honest, because this process only works when you are honest with yourself! First, I started blaming the customer _I_ sold to, because he set me up with the police. Then I blamed society for the obstacles that came from _me_ having a criminal record. I tried to blame everyone and everything externally when the root of the problem was internal.

After I finished shifting responsibility and couldn't lie to the man in the mirror staring back at me, I had to hold **_myself accountable_** for **_my own_** actions and circumstances. Once I started to question many of the decisions I had made which resulted in disastrous outcomes, I had to deconstruct or break down **_why_** I thought the **_way_** I did. I **_inventoried_** my thoughts, which allowed me to **_identify_** the flaws in my thought process.

A few of the things I recognized were patterns of tradition, whether from family or society. I was a product of the environment I grew up around, and much of how I thought was shaped in poverty, around pimps, players, and hustlers with a "you gotta do whatever it takes to get paid" attitude. Thinking like this requires one to need to make spontaneous decisions that often have detrimental consequences. Inventorying and identifying problematic thought patterns lay the groundwork to begin the next step in the process.

Reprogramming/redirecting

Taking a look at where you are (in prison, on supervision, going through court, etc.) and how you got there. Ask yourself, was alcohol/drugs involved? Was there social pressure, money, anger issues? Can you identify where you could have done something differently? During this process, you have to critically evaluate your current conditions. You have to be honest with yourself and question the choices you made which contributed to your present state of affairs. Think about what or who brought you to the position you find yourself currently in. This is the initial inventory process.

Once you have assessed and inventoried the thoughts that led to the actions. The next step is to **identify the catalysts.** That is, those things that can be considered triggers. Triggers can appear in the form of people, places, or things. For example, bumping into an old client, buddy, crime partner etc., may invoke familiar habits. Any ex-addict that wants to remain clean knows they cannot hang out at the dope house. Identifying your triggers can prevent recidivism. For the majority of us money is a trigger, which can lead to re-offending. Pay attention, the pitfalls are real, however; don't only focus on the negative aspects of life. Also learn to identify and acknowledge positive attributes, accomplishments and strides made along the journey. Did you get your GED or diploma? Have you taken parenting, anger management or criminal thinking classes? Maybe you took time to learn how to cook or do maintenance while incarcerated. These are all accomplishments worthy of accolades and praise.

Victim mentality causes one to avoid culpability by shifting accountability to others.

So be humbly proud of yourself. It's okay to celebrate yourself! If you don't, who will?

Reflection Section

1. Inventory & identify areas in your thought process that may cause you to re-offend? List them here.

2. What triggers have you *identified?* People? Places? Things?

Reflection Notes

R. Redirect/Reprogram

Once you have inventoried your thought process, the next step is to acknowledge the flaws in your own thought pattern and decide to reprogram those patterns and redirect your thoughts.

For me it became, think about myself first. I put loyalty over love, and frenemies before family. Who suffers the most when you get locked down? Your parents? Your kids? Your girl/wife? Not only that but, in terms of success vs failure, where do you stand? Calculate the amount of money made, vs amount of time working for that money and now the time sitting. Is it worth it? (Not for me I lost a lot while in prison.) Do I regret the consequences? My 21-year-old nephew was brutally slain while I was sitting in Dodge!

I had to reassess my priorities, and in order to succeed, I had to find my purpose and strategize how to balance personal and professional life.

Find your purpose and pursue it with passion then you can begin to see where you're trying to go. For me it was through my affiliations and work with different churches, and outreach agencies; along with school, which allowed me to find my purpose. My desire has always been to work in the Social Services field and more specifically with Returning Citizens. What can you do to ensure that you never go to prison again? How does being locked up affect your family/friends? What is most important to you? Are you willing to continue to miss out on special occasions and events? Have you ever had family members that died while you were locked-up? How did you feel? Really leaning into these questions will leave you little choice but to reassess your priorities, and hopefully begin to strategize your plans for success upon release!

What plans do you need to devise in order to improve your life? Planning is crucial to the rehabilitation process. You need an exit plan from DOC, you need a plan to start over after release. Most reincarcerations happen within the first 5 years of release. Oftentimes, we feel compelled to try and make up for all we missed out on while we were locked up (i.e., fashion, technology, club life/partying or just enjoying life), so we end up moving too fast or making the wrong moves which sends us back to prison.

Therefore, the importance of reprogramming your mind and how you operate cannot be stressed enough! How do you do time? T.V.? Gym? Dayroom? Are any of these activities going to assist you in not returning to prison? For me, I realized my 2nd time around I had fallen into the "home away from home" or "vacation" mentality which means I allowed myself to become comfortable in subhuman conditions. My last incarceration I bought books instead of a TV, running shoes instead of a radio. I read books, instead of playing cards or dominoes.

Are you trying to elevate your life? How are you going to accomplish this? By reprogramming the way you operate. Remember, plans take time to manifest so you can't rush to catch up once you get out.

The thoughts we entertain now become the actions of the future so when thoughts based in negativity arise (as they will), redirect those thoughts immediately! We must uproot the seeds of negativity before they have a chance to grow into a giant thornbush!

I had to reprogram how I dressed, my choices in women, friends, and my overall appearance. I started to consider what message I wanted to convey even without speaking! Reprogram your networks, resources, and acquaintances around your plans for success. I realized I couldn't see myself being the person

I desired while still remaining connected to many of my past companions. They were still living the life that didn't fit into my future. This is where you have to determine what you want for you. Reprogramming and redirecting lays the foundation to begin the next step in this module: Envision/empower

Life is like chess; the winner is the one with the best strategy!

Reflection Section

1. Explain the difference between reprogramming and redirecting?

2. Describe a situation where you redirected your thoughts.

3. How does being incarcerated affect your loved ones?

Reflection Notes

E. Envision/Empower

In order for your plan to reach any level of success, you must envision attaining that success. You have to see yourself where you want to be, being the person you desire to become and doing what it takes to achieve that success. This is the (in-vision) process, where you examine, enhance, and improve on desired characteristics, attitudes, and behaviors that accentuate the person you are becoming.

While I was in prison, I envisioned myself getting released, but I also envisioned returning to talk to other prisoners about how to get out and stay out. Now, that's what I do in real life. Now that you have devised a strategy, it is time to empower yourself through envisioning yourself as already being where you are trying to go. In other words, "If the mind can conceive it, and the heart can believe it, then the body can achieve it." We are only bound by the restrictions of our own minds. I can recall several instances where I first thought to myself, "I would like to work at this place" and I ended up working there. I recall saying, "The next time I go to prison I'll be leaving on my own terms." I spoke about this program, my agency and everything I have or have had. I spoke them all into existence. You, me (we) must only use words that will empower us, because so much negativity has already been spoken over our lives.

What do you aspire to be? Speak that into your life. If you want to be a better father, say that. Here's an example: "I know I have more to do to become a better _____ (fill in the blank), but I see some improvement." Or "I'm going to become wealthy from starting a lawn-care business." The importance of speaking positive affirmations cannot be stressed enough. If you believe you are a CEO, you are and will become a CEO. Envision yourself being disentangled with the DOC. Imagine yourself filling out the articles of incorporation for your business. Envision your future success and empower yourself to accomplish the task. These two components are intricately linked to your success, but more importantly they are related to self-esteem building. The more you envision yourself as being successful, the more empowered you will become. Being empowered is the realization that you, and you alone determine whether you succeed or fail. You are empowering yourself to be able to accomplish the plans that you established earlier. The manifestation of your empowerment will be found in the future steps, specifically your level of commitment.

Envision (in vision) The vision that lies within you. The way you see yourself will empower you to succeed.

Reflection Section

1. Describe how you envision your future?

2. Explain how accomplishing your vision will empower you.

3. What is one result of envisioning?

Reflection Notes

C. Construct/Commit

This is where you begin to construct a concrete course of actionable items and lay the foundation for the future plans you have established. Here is where you outline and prioritize your plans. If the end goal is to discharge and have your own business, how will you get there? If you are in prison, what opportunities can you take advantage of that will benefit you upon release? Are you employable? Do you need to build your skillset? This is where you put together a solid plan and commit to seeing it through with the understanding that it is going to require sacrifice and commitment. In prison, it may mean more library and research hours and less gym, games, T.V. etc. On the streets, it may mean working and going to school, instead of hanging out.

Commit yourself to transforming as much as you committed yourself to your prior lifestyle. Let's use the construction analogy to describe the process of construct and commit. The architect designs the blueprints or the layout of how the new project will look upon completion. Once the blueprints are approved, the contractor begins by laying the foundation. Therefore, the foundation must be reinforced and fortified to withstand the weight of the structure. Once the foundation is laid and solidified, the contractor then builds upon that foundation, framing, installation, electrical, plumbing, HVAC etc. The project can fail if the architect's blueprints are off, or if the contractor misses a step the project may end in disaster. This is why proper planning, attention to detail and commitment to execution are critical to the successful building of your future.

Failing to plan is equivalent to planning to fail! Practice the 5 P's Proper Planning Prevents Poor Performance!

Reflection Section

1. List at least 2 future plan ideas that you have constructed.

2. In your own words, describe how committed you are to being successful. Why?

Reflection Notes

O. Organize/Objectives

Now that you know where you want to go, have established, and prioritized your plans, you have to organize a timeline complete with objectives. It may look something like:

Upon release within the first 6 months:
1. Find housing
2. Enroll in school for GED/Diploma/Certificate
3. Find a job - start a business (lawn care)
4. Take parenting classes.

You create and organize objectives for as far out on the calendar as you are able to reasonably plan. A 6-month, 1-year and 5-year plan. As you can see, every step is a continuation of the previous step. (For me, my timeline for the completion of school, 3 years, coincided with my discharge from DOC. I strategically planned it that way, which was my objective for 2013.)

Being organized was an easier task for me, simply due to the regimented living conditions of incarceration. Organization is also a process that you do with your mind and thoughts. Many times, I found my mind running away with various thoughts, some thoughts of success, and many of failure. I began organizing the way I saw myself, my vision, and my future, not with the negative lens that I had come to view myself through, but I began thinking of myself in the light of who I am destined to be, not who I was.

O. ORGANIZE/OBJECTIVES

Objective – The operative word here is object. The objective you set for yourself should be an object which you are able to see yourself being consumed with. If your objective is to start your own business, you need to be consumed with learning all you can about the business, the industry, data, and statistical analysis etc. An objective differs from a plan because the plan is the blueprint, the objective is the final outcome.

<u>Your focus on your objective will determine your success! Remember your main objective is success! Organize ideas, thoughts, plans and actions around being successful!</u>

Reflection Section

1. How does being organized work in your favor?

2. Write down your *main* objective after completing this module?

Reflection Notes

G. Generate/Goals

The importance of this aspect cannot be emphasized enough! When establishing your goals, it is best to set short-term and long-term goals. Your goals should always be realistic and attainable. In prison, for instance, one of my goals was to purchase books instead of a television. Why? The books I bought added knowledge and information about things I was interested in doing once I was released.

Goals that are written down and have a completion date provide daily visual motivation. A goal can be as simple as not catching a ticket/violation/new case. In today's society and economy, you have to generate ideas and set financial goals in order to succeed. What goals have you set to attain as a returning citizen? Are you tech-savvy? Do you possess automotive repair skills? How can you transfer these skills and attributes into entrepreneurial opportunities?

Another aspect of setting goals in relation to reducing recidivism is, a person looking forward to being a homeowner or business owner isn't willing to lose any of these or their freedom. Goal generation also works as a barometer, it allows you the ability to see where you were in relation to where you are currently. It also keeps you focused on your future goals. Hope and confidence become increased when goals are met. The longer you focus on succeeding in your goals the less time you will have to engage in criminal thoughts, behaviors, and actions. Remember, routine becomes habit and habit becomes lifestyle. Write it down, keep it where you have to see it daily, on the bathroom mirror, the front door, or the refrigerator are all good places.

I. R.E.C.O.G.N.I.Z.E.

Keep your eyes one the prize!

Reflection Section

1. What are 3 short term goals that you have generated?

2. What are 3 long term goals?

3. How will accomplishing these goals help you to succeed?

Reflection Notes

N. Negotiate/Networks

Life is all about networking and negotiating. Understand that having the best strategies means nothing if you don't have a strong network to assist you on your journey to success. The process of building networks begins right where you are, even in prison. Search for opportunities that may serve dual purposes (i.e., serv-safe certifications, maintenance, etc.). These opportunities provide a temporary escape from the mundane housing life. They also offer the possibility to obtain positive references for your portfolio.

As a returning citizen, networking with volunteering agencies or local religious organizations provides access to various resources and opportunities that will prove invaluable as you build your portfolio. The negotiation comes into play when it becomes necessary to determine and prioritize time management, scheduling priorities and the amount of participation required. Balancing work, family, volunteering, and personal time can be strenuous, which is why you must become adept at negotiating. You might negotiate with your spouse about vacation destinations, your children about their curfew, we may negotiate pay increases or bill payments. Life is full of negotiations; you must be willing to negotiate with others as well as yourself. You must not be so rigid with your plan that you leave no room for adjustment; that is how you negotiate with yourself.

It's not about what you know, it's about who you know! Get to people who can assist you to succeed.

Reflection Section

1. How can those within your network assist you in being successful?

2. Do you need to develop a new network? Why or why not?

Reflection Notes

I. Investigation/Implementation

The investigative step is an analytical critique of your plans with regard to their implementation. You will look to ensure that all goals have been organized and met, networks identified, and that you have a sharp vision of your anticipated outcome(s).

As we all know life is unpredictable, therefore it is always a good practice to plan for unexpected obstacles. Implementation begins once you commit to the rehabilitation process; you must start doing the work! From the time you begin to identify those thoughts, patterns, and behaviors, you must start working to transform them and yourself in order to position yourself for success. Implementation may require disassociation from friends and associates that have a negative impact on your objectives. Begin implementing your strategy by obtaining training and certifications where you are.

The ultimate aim is to build a portfolio of your life complete with criminal history and positive achievements. This gives you the ability to actually see your transformation and show it to others. Again, I will use an analogy in reference to chess.

Examine and re-examine your strategy, *and the board before making a move!* When you stay ready, you don't have to get ready!

Reflection Section

1. Have you identified potential obstacles during the investigation phase?

2. How confident are you in your plans?

Reflection Notes

Z. Zealously/Zero In

Now is the time to zero in on the future you desire and put all of your energy, passion, tenacity, and trust in your vision. To be zealous means that you are like the lead car in the Nascar 500, you are racing for the finish line, pursuing that coveted trophy, and you won't let anyone, or anything stop you except that checkered flag.

To zero in means you have tunnel vision, like a horse that has blinders on. The blinders keep the horse from seeing what's going on around it but allow the horse to focus straight ahead. That is how you zero in and zealously pursue your success.

Move with purpose. Aggressively pursue your dreams! If your mind can conceive it; your heart can believe it, you can achieve it!

Reflection Section

1. Success is the target, and you *will not be denied!*

2. Move with a sense of urgency and purpose.

Reflection Notes

E. Emerge/Execute

Whether you are coming out of the dayroom or the institution these two things will determine your level of success. You have to show up and execute your plans to change. You are like a caterpillar, the time you have isolated from family and friends is your metamorphosis phase. The prison is your cocoon. When you emerge you can either be a beautiful butterfly flying in the light and warmth of the sun to your highest heights, or you can emerge a moth relegated to the darkness chasing the heat and light of a lamp! All of your earlier steps have brought you to this stage. You have identified the thoughts and actions that led to your incarceration. In response, you have reformed your thought process to envision yourself succeeding and constructed and organized a goal-driven course of action. Networking has become a customary practice in your everyday life.

Now as you emerge it is time to zero in on your future, use your past as stepping stones and go out and **MANifest your destiny!**

Reflection Section

As I reflect on October 24th, 2009, my release date, I'm reminded of all the obstacles, tragedies, failures, and barriers that I was faced with. I even ended up in a MAX holding facility while being investigated for a crime I didn't commit and had to sit for 2 weeks doing 23 hours in a cell with 1 hour out. I'm saying this to demonstrate unforeseen situations will come to throw you off the path, that's when you go *back to the plan!* My P.O. eventually released me, but I had missed several opportunities I had created for myself.

Now I personally want to thank each and every person that has taken the time to pour over the material contained within these pages. My desire is that by applying the principles in this module your transformation will be evident to you as well as others. I pray that others use this module to achieve success in their personal and professional lives.

I am proud of you for committing yourself to change for the better. I know you can accomplish whatever you set out to do. Never doubt yourself, just *know you* are destined to win in the end!

Reflection Notes

Reflection Notes

Reflection Notes

Reflection Notes

Reflection Notes

Reflection Notes

Reflection Notes

Reflection Notes

Reflection Notes

Reflection Notes

Reflection Notes

www.ingramcontent.com/pod-product-compliance
Lightning Source LLC
Chambersburg PA
CBHW060034180426
43196CB00045B/2685